FROM THE
Dead Sea Scrolls
TO THE
Bible in America

A Brief History of the Bible
From Antiquity to Modern America

Told through Ancient Manuscripts and
Early European and American Printed Bibles

By Lee Biondi

Ethiopic St. Mark (Ethiopia 15th Century)

From the Dead Sea Scrolls to the Bible in America

ISBN 978-0-9792877-2-5
© 2009 Legacy Ministries International

Published by Spire Resources, Inc.
PO Box 180, Camarillo, CA 93011

Printed in the United States of America

FROM THE
Dead Sea Scrolls
TO THE
Bible in America

PREFACE

This exhibition has been put together to tell a dramatic and inspirational story—the story of how we got the Bible. And more specifically, how we got the Bible in English and how the Bible was influential in establishing and shaping the United States of America.

This is a story of faith, dedication and sacrifice—for many, the ultimate sacrifice of being martyred for one's belief in God and Holy Scripture.

The Jews of Qumran, whose caves housed what we now call the Dead Sea Scrolls, were slaughtered by the Romans for their beliefs and their sacred writings. So, too, were many early Christians for their efforts in spreading Holy Scripture. Many of the scholars who translated the Bible into English were murdered as heretics by Church and State authorities. Such was the fate of William Tyndale, John Rogers and Thomas Cranmer. John Wyclif, the first translator of the Bible into English, died a natural death but was later exhumed by order of Church authorities who *burned his bones* and denounced him as a heretic.

What we might take for granted—that Bible in English on our desk or bedside table, or in the bookrack of a church pew—is the result of thousands of years of struggle.

This exhibition is unusual in its range and scope. Though previous exhibits around the world have dealt with certain portions of the story in greater depth, few have attempted the telling of the full history by displaying genuine examples of every phase of the story from the very earliest Bible fragments in existence to the first Bible that went to the Moon.

Presented as a prelude to this exhibition of Holy Scripture are artifacts that show the origins of writing—items from the earliest type of writing known to man, pictography, dating back 5,000 years to the Sumerian culture of Mesopotamia (modern-day Iraq). These proto-cuneiform and cuneiform examples point to the invention of alphabets, the development that made possible the effective communication of lengthy works and complex thoughts.

Dead Sea Scroll
Fragment of Psalms

The first part of the exhibition covers the *manuscript* tradition of Scripture from handwritten fragments of ancient Hebrew Bibles up to the invention of the printing press.

On exhibit are authentic, Scriptural Dead Sea Scroll fragments—ancient Hebrew examples of the earliest known witnesses to the Hebrew Bible (The *Tanakh*, The Old Testament). Like so many of the scrolls, these have broken apart and darkened over the ages. Their text can be read only through infrared photography. Professional translations by Israeli scholars familiar with scripts of the period accompany each fragment on display.

The discovery of the Dead Sea Scrolls, in the years after World War II, is the most important discovery ever made in the study of Biblical texts.

In the 19th Century scholars began to question the extent to which the modern world could rely upon the textual tradition of the Hebrew Bible since existing manuscripts could not be traced any further back than the 10th and early 11th Centuries. The discovery of the Dead Sea Scrolls suddenly pushed the existing manuscript tradition more than a thousand years further back into ancient history. As these books of the Hebrew Bible were thoroughly studied, the fact emerged that the manuscript tradition had been miraculously accurate.

Caves of Qumran

As Greek became the main language of the entire region of the Holy Land and Egypt, the Hebrew Bible had to be translated into Greek in order to continue as a living text. The ancient rendering of Holy Scripture into Greek is called the Septuagint, abbreviated in Roman numerals as LXX ("70"), because of the traditional story of its having been rendered by 70 (or sometimes 72) translators. In fact, it was the work of several generations of Jewish translators, originally based in Alexandria, Egypt, from the middle 3rd Century B.C. to the late 2nd Century B.C. Depicted on the next page is a fragment of a 4th Century Book of Exodus on papyrus contemporaneous with the great Septuagint manuscripts known as the *Codex Vaticanus* (now in the Vatican Library) and the *Codex Sinaiticus* (now in the British Library). These are the earliest witnesses to the Septuagint version of the Bible.

During this period early Christians developed the modern book form, called a *codex*, which is bound with pages that turn. This development was a great practical advance over the ancient world's reliance on the scroll form.

The Septuagint Greek version of Holy Scripture was often read and studied by early Christians, and was the version predominantly quoted by New Testament authors when citing the Old Testament.

As Greek had dominated the region after the conquests of Alexander the Great, Latin came to dominate after the expansion of the Roman Empire. Latin translations of uneven quality began to circulate, and the Church determined that a comprehensive standardized translation was needed.

Septuagint fragment, 4th Century A.D.

Jerome, translator of the Latin Vulgate

In the late 4th Century A.D. Bishop Damasus of Rome commissioned the greatest scholar of the period, Jerome, to produce a definitive version of both the Old Testament and the New Testament in Latin. The version that Jerome delivered became known as the Vulgate, the standard version of the complete Bible in Latin which dominated through the Dark and Middle Ages.

By the end of the 12th Century, the Vulgate Bible had been compiled into the physical form we now know as "The Bible" with the various books of the Bible divided into standard numbered chapters (but not yet into numbered verses). This medieval Bible tradition is exemplified in leaves from

John Wyclif, translator of the Latin Vulgate into English

13th Century Bibles and Books of Hours, devotional works produced mainly by Dominican and Franciscan friars who instigated these developments.

The first time the Bible was translated into English, the text was based on the Latin Vulgate. This first translation was accomplished in the circle of the greatest English theologian of the 14th Century, a Doctor of Theology at Oxford named John Wyclif (now commonly written as Wycliffe), who is rightfully remembered as

"The Morningstar of the Reformation." By the time of Wyclif's death in 1384, an "Early Version" of the Bible in English was complete. This version was a stilted rendering, awkward in English because of its literal word-for-word translation. A more "user-friendly" rendering in Middle English was quickly delivered by Wyclif's followers.

Between the time of these Wycliffite manuscript Bibles and the time of the first editions of Scripture by Martin Luther and William Tyndale, the printing press had been invented. The history of the dissemination of Scripture was forever changed—which takes us to the second half of this exhibition: the history of the Bible *in print*.

In the middle of the 15th Century, Johannes Gutenberg invented the printing press using moveable type. Appropriately, his first major undertaking was to print the full Latin Bible. The Gutenberg Bible is a hinge point of this exhibition and is one of the most important moments in human history. No longer would every Bible have to be slowly and painstakingly written by hand. Editions of Holy Scripture could be printed by the hundreds and even the thousands. With every passing year, more and more laypersons were able to acquire their own copy of God's Word. As this occurred, these very readers longed for a Bible not just in Latin, but in their own vernacular languages, so they could absorb and contemplate Holy Scripture in a more convenient and understanding way.

Though they suffered great persecution, Martin Luther, William Tyndale and Cassiodoro de Reina began to provide Holy Scripture to believers in their native languages. For their work in bringing Scripture to English-speaking believers, William Tyndale, John Rogers and Thomas Cranmer were burned at the stake. Many others suffered exile. Our exhibition brings together every important early phase of the history of the printed Bible in Greek, Latin, German, Spanish and English. Major English translations are represented from an early Tyndale version to the "Geneva" version of William Whittingham to the Anglican "Bishops' Bible" of Matthew Parker to the summit of English Bible publishing: the grand pulpit folio of the 1611 King James Bible.

The story may reach its summit at the King James Bible of 1611, but not its conclusion. The history of the Bible in America is also deserving of our attention. It was a violation of King's copyright to print a Bible in English in Colonial America—and Colonial printers were not granted the King's privilege to print Bibles. Scriptures at that time had to be imported from England, Scotland or Holland. The first Scripture to be printed in America was a missionary Bible in the Natick Algonquian Indian dialect, published in 1663 and known as "Eliot's Indian Bible" after its translator John Eliot, one of the greatest missionaries in American history. No Bible in English would be printed in America until after our Declaration

*William Tyndale, first translator of the English
Bible from the original languages*

of Independence. In 1782 Robert Aitken, official printer to Congress, published his Bible, a King James Version proudly called among the populace "The Bible of the Revolution." Displayed in this exhibition is a first edition of this Bible alongside the official Congressional Declaration supporting its publication and recommending this edition of the Bible to "all inhabitants of the United States."

The exhibition also includes examples from every important early American Bible, each a reminder of the strong faith of our founding fathers, and the Christian principles upon which this nation was built.

The preservation, transmission and translation of Holy Scripture has been a long and difficult struggle. It is one that must continue until everyone in the world who desires to read Scripture has ready access to a Bible in his or her native language.

All of us involved in organizing this unique exhibition hope that it will have a *living* purpose beyond merely assembling these fine and rare museum artifacts. Our deeper desire is that this exhibition would actively remind us that the task of spreading the Word of God is not yet fully accomplished, that the dissemination of Holy Scripture is still a work-in-progress, and that we must carry that work forward with all diligence.

"All Scripture is God-breathed and is useful..."
II Timothy, 3:16

4th Century fragment from Book of Exodus

THE ORIGINS OF WRITING

Mesopotamian pictography, circa 2400 B.C.

Examples of some of the earliest surviving pieces of writing are displayed as a prologue to the history of Holy Scripture, to show how written languages developed.

Featured in the exhibition is the earliest form of human writing—pictography—which was a precursor of the ancient cuneiform system of writing that was developed by the Sumerian culture in Mesopotamia (modern-day Iraq) over 5,000 years ago. In pictography, the pictures stand for what they represent quite literally. On display are several examples concerning everyday events and transactions such as the sale of livestock and a payroll tally. Pictography has obvious limitations in the complexity of thought that can be accurately expressed by the writer and understood by the eventual reader.

Sumerian cuneiform literary tablet, 2nd Millennium B.C.

Development of a phonetic form of writing was inevitable for the act of memorializing spoken languages within a writing system. Some types of pictography developed into abstract writing closer to our alphabet of today, using symbols to represent sounds (phonemes or syllables). Cuneiform is such a system of writing that can express several languages with one system of writing, but it is not as refined as the modern alphabet. Most languages expressed in cuneiform required several hundred symbols, rendering it much more unwieldy than our current twenty-six letter alphabet. As economic systems and the general culture of Mesopotamia developed, scribes invented this form of writing as a way to express complex thoughts in many of the region's languages. Cuneiform was written in wet clay, in a series of tiny shapes formed by the

Cuneiform Scribal School tablet, 2nd Millennium B.C.

11

Mesopotamian cuneiform, circa 2nd Millennium B.C.

distinctive wedged stylus used to make the impressions. Cuneiform means "wedge-shaped." It is no longer pictographic, though developed from pictographs, and it represents a huge and important leap forward in human ability to record and transmit complex thoughts.

Other early forms of ancient writing included Egyptian hieroglyphics, Chinese ideograms, and the Indus Valley script (which remains undeciphered). These originated as pictograms, but also developed into phonemes and syllables to

Chinese oracle bone, circa 1800 B.C.   *Indus Valley seal, circa 2200 B.C.*

Egyptian Book of the Dead fragment, circa 1st Millennium B.C.

Ancient Roman wax tablet book, single wooden leaf,
now with later Coptic Psalm written in ink

express thoughts and meaning beyond their simpler pictorial representations. Egyptian hieroglyphs are phonetic in operation, despite their pictorial nature, and any text in hieroglyphs could also be expressed in a script form known as Hieratic.

With the exception of the region of Ugarit, which cleverly developed cuneiform into a locally used proto-alphabet, the North Semitic scripts were the first to generalize the usage of an alphabet that would be recognizable as such to moderns. These North Semitic scripts utilized thirty or fewer constituent signs. The word "alphabet" derives from the first two signs: *aleph* and *bet* (in Hebrew) or *alpha* and *beta* in the Greek. This formative alphabet, which dates to the first half of the 2nd Millennium B.C., is the basis for Canaanitic writing, which in turn evolved into the Moabite, Edomite, early Paleo-Hebrew, later "square" Hebrew, and Phoenician scripts. The Greeks subsequently borrowed mostly from the Phoenician version and in turn transmitted their alphabet to the Latins and Etruscans.

Extraordinary fragment in Greek on Papyrus, 3rd Century A.D., identifiable as from Homer's Iliad

Ancient Greek on Papyrus, circa 2nd or 3rd Century A.D., with example of an interlinear correction

THE MANUSCRIPT TRADITION OF HOLY SCRIPTURE

*Fragment from the Paleo-Hebrew Leviticus Scroll under
natural light (11QPaleoLev, fragment L)*

The Dead Sea Scroll Fragments

The earliest surviving authentic Biblical texts are a few scrolls and hundreds of fragments of scrolls that were discovered between 1947 and 1956 in the Qumran caves near the Dead Sea, and which are known collectively as "The Dead Sea

Fragment from the Dead Sea Scroll Wisdom Text 4Q418 (4QInstruction)

Scrolls." These manuscripts date from about 250 B.C. to no later than 68 A.D., the date that the Jewish community at Qumran was overrun and destroyed by the Roman army. The great collections of Dead Sea Scroll manuscripts and fragments reside permanently at the Shrine of the Book and the Rockefeller Museum in

Facing Page: St. Jerome, translator of the manuscript Latin Vulgate Bible

15

Jerusalem, and, to a lesser extent, at the *Bibliotheque Nationale* in Paris. The texts at the Shrine of the Book are sometimes on display to the public, though the great scroll of Isaiah is no longer shown except in facsimile. Rarely are any fragments shown outside Israel and even more rarely are fragments shown in the context of the overall history of the English Bible. The Biblical fragments on display in this exhibition are in Hebrew, from the Old Testament. Like most of the surviving fragments, these have darkened so much over the last 2,000 years that sophisticated infrared photography is needed to reveal the handwriting.

A Dead Sea Scroll Fragment of Psalm 11 under infrared light

A Dead Sea Scroll Fragment of Exodus

The Dead Sea Scrolls constitute the greatest discovery ever made in the field of Biblical textual studies. This discovery took the manuscript tradition of the Hebrew Bible over a thousand years further back into ancient history, and ended doubts about the accuracy of the textual transmission of the Hebrew Scriptures from antiquity to the medieval world. The Dead Sea Scrolls have been very reassuring on this point as the ancient beginnings of the Bible have been finally and indisputably set in a secure context. Before the discovery of the Dead Sea Scrolls, the earliest known Hebrew Biblical manuscripts were from the 10th Century A.D. and the earliest complete Hebrew Bible [*Codex Leningradensis*] was from about the year 1000 A.D. [Note 1] — whereas the Dead Sea Scrolls can be accurately dated to circa 250 B.C. to 68 A.D. The discovery of the Dead Sea Scrolls effectively put to rest any argument about the fact that certain prophecies were written before the lifetime of Jesus (as had been claimed about the prophetic writings of Isaiah and Daniel).

In 1947, a young shepherd named Mazra from the Ta'amireh tribe of Bedouins inadvertently made this great discovery by throwing a rock into a little cave entrance and, upon hearing the shattering of pottery, decided to explore further. From this first cave, the Bedouin retrieved seven substantial scrolls, including the most important single manuscript discovery in the world: the great Isaiah scroll now at the Shrine of the Book in Jerusalem, the only complete text found in any of the Dead Sea caves and the text that most impressively bears testimony to the integrity of the Jewish scribal tradition from Second Temple Period to the medieval world. These major scrolls went from the Bedouin to the Metropolitan

View of the ruins of Qumran

(Archbishop) of the local Syrian Orthodox Church and to Professor Sukenik of the Hebrew University of West Jerusalem. [Note 2] At this time there was no nation of Israel; the area was the British Mandate of Palestine. On May 14, 1948, Israel declared its independent status as a new nation and the first Arab-Jewish War officially began the very next day. The ceasefire and truce were arranged in January of 1949. There were no new discoveries until the Bedouin found Cave 2 in February of 1952. Authorized scholars from the *Ecole Biblique*, the Palestine Museum (later the Rockefeller) and the American School of Oriental Research found Cave 3 in March of the same year, but were beaten to the amazingly productive Cave 4 by the Bedouin in September. The officials stepped in while the Bedouin were clearing out Cave 4, so some of these fragments went onto the private market and some went immediately under Jordanian control. It was Cave 4 that produced the highest number of fragments. Cave 5 was found by the official team; Cave 6 by the Bedouin; Caves 7-10 by the team; and Cave 11, the final productive cave, by the Bedouin in 1956.

The Ritual Bath (Mikveh) at Qumran

These discoveries were all made during a period when Jordan claimed sovereignty over the West Bank. Jordan retained possession of the West Bank until the Six Day War of 1967, won by Israel.

The seven original discoveries from Cave 1 are now in the possession of the Nation of

Israel and are housed at the beautiful Shrine of the Book in Jerusalem. The Rockefeller Museum (formerly the Palestine Museum) has most of the other pieces that are held by institutions in the Mid-East, with a few pieces at the Museum of the Department of Antiquities in Amman, Jordan. Those fragments that went to the *Ecole Biblique* are now at the *Bibliotheque Nationale.* By their occupation, Israeli jurisdiction of the Rockefeller Museum (the Palestine Archaeological Museum), like that of the West Bank, is not uncontested, though the situation is settled. All of the Dead Sea Scroll fragments in this exhibition are from various privately-held collections around the world; none of the material is from any museum or other institution.

The community of Essene Jews who lived at Qumran had an efficient scriptorium and probably functioned as a "publishing house," if you will, for the dissemination of Hebrew Scripture. But not all the manuscripts found in the caves of Qumran were scribed there; the Library at Qumran seems to have been representative of a great deal of Second Temple Period texts, some that were probably quite old even when the community first settled the area. Some of the Scripture found at Qumran was written in an ancient form of Hebrew lettering called Paleo-Hebrew, such as the well-known Paleo-Leviticus scroll that is mostly now at the Rockefeller Museum.

It is commonly reported that at least a fragment of "every book of the Old Testament was found in the Dead Sea Scrolls except Esther." This is true if speaking from a Jewish perspective as, indeed, every book of the *Tanakh* was found but Esther. But the Tanakh considers Ezra and Nehemiah as a single book and nothing was found from the Nehemiah portion—that is, until the identification and trans-

Ruins of the Qumran Community

A Dead Sea Scroll Fragment of Exodus

lation of the Nehemiah fragment in this exhibition. From the Catholic perspective a different view arises as only Tobit, Sirach (same as the Protestant/Anglican Book of "Ecclesiasticus"), and Letter of Jeremiah, were found at Qumran from the Catholic "Deuterocanonical" books, roughly equivalent to the Protestant and Anglican "Apocrypha" (please see Appendix for more information on the canons of Scripture). The disputed Psalm 151 was also found at Qumran.

Aside from the directly Biblical texts found at Qumran, the texts of the greatest interest are the commentaries on Scripture (called *Midrash* or *Pesharim*) and a genre called the Wisdom Texts, or the Sapiential Texts. The most prominent literary form among the sapiential texts from Qumran is the "wisdom instruction." The most extensive wisdom instruction text from the Dead Sea Scrolls is known to the scholarly community as Sapiential Work A or 4QInstruction (titled and published for popular consumption as "The Secret of the Way Things Are" by Wise, Abegg, and Cook in their new edition, *The Dead Sea Scrolls: a New Translation*, 1996), appearing in six fragmentary copies (1Q26, 4Q415-418, and 423). The three main topics of this text are money and possessions, social relations, and family matters. The advice on these three topics is punctuated by exhortations to study and contemplate the "*raz nihyeh*" ("the mystery that is to be"). The student who meditates on the *raz nihyeh* is promised ethical knowledge, understanding of creation, and a glimpse of the future. Sapiential Work A appeals to the threat of eschatological ("end times") judgment as a motive for wise and righteous behavior in the present. Its posing of a "mystery that is to be" or "mystery that is to become" could lead to a theological, or at least philosophical, linkage with the Gnostic sect that thrived in the early centuries after Christ. Scholars also link this Wisdom Text, or Instruction Text to the Second Temple literary genres of Apocalyptic, or eschatological works.

To date, there have been no discoveries at Qumran from any works of the New Testament, though there are some resonances in certain themes and even some wordings.

The Septuagint

The Septuagint is the name of the first translation of Hebrew Holy Scripture into another language: Greek. After the conquests of Alexander the Great during the 4th Century B.C., Greek became the predominant language of commerce and

*Fragments from a
4th Century A.D.
Septuagint on Papyrus
(Exodus)*

culture throughout the Middle East and Egypt and many Jews became more conversant in Greek than in Hebrew.

The Septuagint was generated by Jews of the dispersion in Alexandria, Egypt for their own usage, and this translation became Holy Scripture for Hellenistic Judaism outside of Judea.

The Septuagint is accompanied by several legends. Tradition has it that the work was commissioned by Ptolemy II Philadelphus of Egypt for inclusion in the great library at Alexandria; but in fact the translation was a product of Jewish community needs, not of imperial desires. Tradition further has it that the translation is called the Septuagint—which means "Seventy"—because 70 (sometimes 72) translators working in isolation generated identical renderings. In truth, the work was accomplished over several generations during the 3rd and early 2nd Centuries B.C.

The Septuagint became the Holy Scripture for the Early Christian Church. When New Testament writers cite Holy Scripture from the Old Testament, over eighty percent of the quotes can be identified as coming from the Septuagint version.

The Septuagint text was, in effect, the Word of God for the first three centuries of the Church. As such, its inclusion of the "Deuterocanonical" Books (the Protestant Apocrypha) helped determine the canonical status of this body of books and additions to books that were denied canonical status by 2nd Century Rabbinical Jews. [Note 3]

These papyrus fragments from Exodus date to the mid-4th Century A.D., contemporaneous with the two greatest surviving Septuagint manuscripts: *Codex Sinaiticus* (at the British Museum) and *Codex Vaticanus* (in the Vatican Library).

 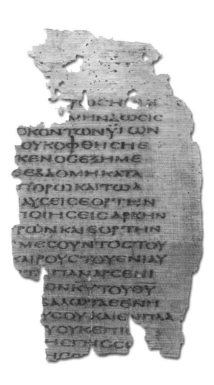

It should be noted that these fragments above are leaves from a handwritten *book*, not fragments of *scrolls*, and they contain portions of Exodus in Greek that are not otherwise extant on papyrus.

The Early New Testament

Paul's Epistle to the Colossians

The hugely important New Testament fragment depicted on page 23 provides one of the earliest witnesses anywhere in the world to any of Paul's Letters to the Early Churches. The text surviving is from Colossians 3:21-4:7 on the recto (front) and 4:7-15 on the verso (back). Written on papyrus in the Egyptian language called Coptic, it is datable to the 3rd Century A.D. and is wonderful evidence of the rapid spread of Christian beliefs. It is worth remembering that whatever individuals or groups owned and read from this letter were subjecting themselves to arrest and execution by the soldiers of the Roman Empire, as this was well before Constantine suppressed the martyring of Christians.

Among the most fascinating non-Scriptural antiquities are the so-called "lost gospels" or "secret gospels." Discovered in 1945 in Upper Egypt at a site named Nag Hammadi, this find pre-dated the discovery of the Dead Sea Scrolls by only two years and was similar in that the material was accidentally found by a young Egyptian boy. The details of the two discoveries are often stirred together in the popular imagination but are clearly distinguished in the academic and religious communities. The Dead Sea Scrolls included actual pieces of Old Testament Scripture, but nothing from the New Testament; the Nag Hammadi find was New Testament time period, but not scriptural. The Dead Sea Scrolls were mostly in Hebrew written on skins; the Nag Hammadi find was mostly in Coptic written on papyrus. The Dead Sea Scroll material was of earlier origin, circa 200 B.C. to 68 A.D., whereas the Nag Hammadi material was circa 3rd/4th Centuries A.D. The Dead Sea material was written in scroll format and the Nag Hammadi texts were in book form, called codices. These writings (*The Gospel of Thomas* being the most famous and widely published) were never serious contenders for the Canon of the New Testament; they were deemed heretical as early as during the lifetime of the Church Father Irenaeus in his *Adversus Haereses* (c. 180 A.D.).

The Latin Vulgate Bible

After centuries of cruel suppression by the Romans, Christianity was officially accepted and adopted during the reign of the Roman Emperor Constantine who effectively took control of the empire in the year 312 A.D. after his famous victory at the Milvian Bridge over his main rival Maxentius. At the Battle of Milvian Bridge, Constantine had conquered under the standard known as the *labarum*, or the *Chi-Rho*, the Christian monogram of the first two letters of the name of Christ (X and P) intersecting. Shortly thereafter Constantine granted toleration and even Imperial favor to Christianity. It was Constantine who first made Sunday a legal public holiday. In 313 A.D. the emperors Constantine and Licinius met to co-establish a policy of religious toleration, and, although this meeting marked the triumph of Christianity and the termination of Imperial persecution, it did not officially establish the Church as the official religion of the Empire(s). [Note 4] After Constantine's subsequent victory over Licinius at Chrysopolis in 324 A.D., he fixed his capital at Byzantium, rather than Rome, and in 330 A.D. the city was renamed

Fragment of Paul's Epistle to the Colossians
3rd Century A.D. Written in Coptic, ink on papyrus,
text of Colossians 3:21-4:15

Papyrus fragments from the late New Testament Period showing
a "Gnostic" Creation Story in Coptic, 3rd/4th Century A.D.

Constantinople. Constantine was not baptized in the Christian faith until near the end of his life. He ruled until his death in the year 337. Constantine's transfer of Imperial control from Rome to Constantinople had the consequence of increasing the Imperial control of the Church in the East and of making the bishops of Rome more prominent than any other figures in the West—and it was from the 4th Century that the bishops of Rome began to assume a position of secular, as well as spiritual influence in Europe.

"Gospel of James"
Colophon

Toward the end of the 4th Century A.D., Bishop Damasus of Rome (now known as Pope Damasus) conscripted Jerome (now known as Saint Jerome), the leading scholar of the period, to establish a standard Latin text of the books of the Bible.

Jerome's mandate was to render a new Latin Bible—the established Canon of Holy Scripture—using as sources the original Hebrew for the Old Testament and the original Greek for the New Testament (though much of the Old Testament and the latter books of the

New Testament were retained in Old Latin [*Vetus Latina,* or *Vetus Italica,* or *Itala*] versions or re-translated by others). Wherever possible, Jerome worked from the original Hebrew and Greek manuscripts available to him. The Greek exemplars available to him included the Septuagint and the translations of Aquila, Symmachus and Theodotion through the imposing *Hexapla* of Origen. [Note 5] Jerome's work was completed by the early 5th Century. He rendered three versions of the Psalter (the Book of Psalms), but he did not translate the full established canon of the Church and, therefore, the Vulgate was an uneven final product, and was slow to achieve universal acceptance.

For some of the books of the Septuagint Old Testament, Jerome was unable to find examples in Hebrew. Since he was uneasy about having to render these books into Latin from their earlier translation into Greek (finding himself translating a translation), he created a category for these books and dubbed them "hidden" —using the term "apocrypha." It is worth noting that examples of some of these books of The Apocrypha *were* found in Hebrew with the discovery of the Dead Sea Scrolls (e.g., fragments of Tobit, Ecclesiasticus (Wisdom of Ben Sirach), and the Prayer of Jeremiah). [For a brief essay on the Canon(s) of Scripture(s) and The Apocrypha, please see Appendix.]

Jerome's Latin translation of the Bible (incorporating as stated the Old Latin versions of some portions) became known as the Vulgate, or the *Biblia Latina,* or simply *Biblia Sacra,* and henceforth was the only recognized version of Holy Scripture by the Roman Church. [Note 6] Jerome's Vulgate was soon so highly endorsed and later so dominant that it was not substantially revised by the Vatican until the so-called Clementine revision of 1592. [Note 7]

Book of Hours

Jerome also wrote a series of Prologues to many of the books of the Bible which became a standard feature of many of the medieval manuscript Latin Bibles. As time passed, more and more often the individual books of the Roman canon of the Bible appeared together in a single bound work. This type of one-volume Bible is called a *pandect*. During the late 12th Century the pandect *Biblia*

Latina began to take on the book form by which it is recognized today: exhibiting a standard order of the books and standardized chapter divisions. (Standard versification was a refinement of the 16th Century.)

The period of manuscript Bibles from Carolingian times to the High Renaissance is the period of grand illumination of Bibles, liturgical books, and the glorious examples of Books of Hours—the most prevalent and most consistently beautiful of all medieval and Renaissance manuscripts, the epitome of the Catholic private devotional known as the Hours of the Blessed Virgin Mary.

The Wycliffite Bible in English

John Wyclif (ca. 1329-1384) is rightfully regarded as "The Morningstar of the Reformation." He and his circle at Oxford (whose followers were commonly called Lollards) were the first translators of the full Bible into English. Their Middle English Bible was translated from manuscripts of the Latin Vulgate of Saint Jerome. The "Early Version"—completed by 1384—was extremely literal, almost awkwardly so, and was immediately followed by a more flowing "Later Version." Wyclif (commonly spelled Wycliffe) believed most fervently that Scripture was the only law, and that it should be readily accessible to all citizens. In his *De Ecclesia* and *De Veritate Sacrae Scripturae* Wyclif maintained that the Bible, as the eternal exemplar of the Christian religion should be the sole criterion of doctrine, to which no ecclesiastical authority might lawfully or rightfully add. Wyclif was sufficiently politically protected to survive the ecclesiastical censures against him in 1377, 1378 and 1382. In 1388 and 1397, Wyclif's doctrines and his followers were subjected to further condemnations after his death, and finally at the 1414-1417 Council of Constance by Pope Martin V.

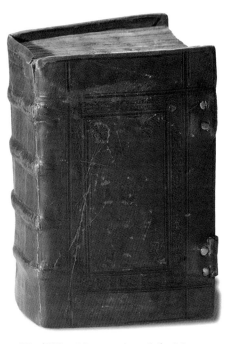

In an official legal act of 1401 (*De Heretico Comburendo*) and a declaration in the year 1409 (the Arundel Constitutions), translating Scripture into English, or even owning or reading an English Bible, could be deemed heretical and an offense punishable by death. [Notes 8 and 9]

Wycliffite Manuscript of the New Testament in English, ca. 1390

26

THE HISTORY OF HOLY SCRIPTURE IN PRINT

The Gutenberg Bible

1455

The first substantial book ever printed in the West was—appropriately—the most important book ever written: *The Holy Bible (Biblia Sacra)*. Johannes Gutenberg, inventor of the art and craft of printing with moveable type, experimented with small projects during the early 1450s. He began his Bible around 1452, probably completing it in Mainz, Germany in 1455, with his partners on the project, Johann Fust and Peter Schoeffer. The text was the standard Vulgate Latin of Saint Jerome, the *Biblia Latina*. This work is known colloquially as "The Gutenberg Bible" and officially among bibliographers as "The 42-line Bible." Amazingly, the first book ever printed remains one of the most beautiful books ever produced, a testimony to the meticulous care and artistry that Johannes Gutenberg applied to the work.

The example below is a leaf from the Book of Isaiah.

After the pioneering work of Gutenberg, Fust, and Schoeffer, the printing revolution spread rapidly across Europe The new technology meant that the Bible was accessible to more and more people, not exclusively the aristocracy and clergy.

Printed books from the Gutenberg Bible to the year 1501 are called *incunabula,* or, in its English form, incunables, meaning "from the cradle [of printing]." Other great early incunable Bibles include the 1460 edition known as "The 36-line Bible" or "The Bamberg Bible" and the 1462 Fust and Schoeffer Bible, the first Bible bearing a date.

The first vernacular Bible to be printed was the Mentelin German Bible of 1466 printed in Strasbourg. It was a decidedly inelegant version of the text, but significant. Deemed heretical, it was influenced by the beliefs of the Waldenses, a sect which renounced the doctrines and usages of the Roman Church as far back as the 12th Century and continued from that point forward to base its faith on Scripture alone. The first Bible in Italian, Malermi's translation, was printed in Venice in 1471 by Vindelinus de Spira. The first complete Hebrew Bible was printed by the renowned Soncino family of publishers in 1488.

The Erasmus New Testament in Greek and Latin

1516

The First New Testament to be published in Greek was the 1516 Froben edition of Desiderius Erasmus of Rotterdam, the leading intellectual of his generation. It was an achievement of the highest order in the history of the printed Bible.

Desiderius Erasmus

His 1519 revised edition was the sourcebook for the Reformation German translation of Martin Luther. The revised 1522 edition was the Greek and Latin sourcebook used by William Tyndale for his new English translation, the first translation of Scripture into English since Wyclif, and the first version to be translated into Modern English directly from the original Biblical languages. Erasmus did not have as intense a theological flame within him as did Martin Luther and William Tyndale, but there is no doubt that his Greek and Latin New Testament was the spark that lit the fires of the Reformation in England and on the Continent. Even more than the *95 Theses* of Luther (1517), it was the advent of Holy Scripture readily available in the vernacular languages of German and English that spread the Reformation in those countries.

The First Tyndale New Testament

1526

After a sabotaged attempt to publish his English New Testament at Cologne in 1525, William Tyndale succeeded in publishing the first edition of Holy Scripture in English with his 1526 New Testament printed in Worms, Germany by Peter Schoeffer, the grandson of the Peter Schoeffer who was assistant and partner to Johannes Gutenberg in Mainz in the 1450s. Only two copies of this hugely important book remain in existence: one in London and one in Stuttgart.

William Tyndale, the greatest translator of Scripture into English who ever lived, was not permitted to finish his work. He was betrayed, arrested, and imprisoned in Vilvoorde Castle in Belgium for 500 days before being strangled to death and burned at the stake for his "crime" of translating Scripture into the English language. Tyndale finished about half of the Old Testament before his martyrdom in 1536. His work was continued in his spirit by the dedicated John Rogers and Miles Coverdale, but it would not be until William Whittingham's work on the 1560 "Geneva" Bible that a scholar sufficiently skilled in the Hebrew language would complete the Old Testament in English directly from the Hebrew text.

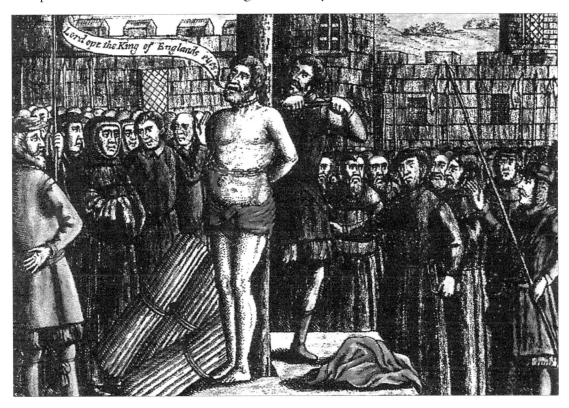

The Martyrdom of William Tyndale, 1536, as depicted in John Foxe, Acts and Monuments of the Christian Church (Foxe's Book of Martyrs)

29

The Reformation German Bible of Martin Luther

1536

Martin Luther was the leading figure of the early Reformation on the European Continent. His "September" New Testament, published in Wittenberg in 1522, and his partial Old Testament of 1523 led to his first complete Bible in German in 1534—a book which had a profound impact on the history of religious thought and the development of the German language. Luther's German New Testament was translated from the Greek of Erasmus, using the second edition. In the list of books given in the preliminary matter, four (Hebrews, James, Jude, and Revelation) are separated from the others and not included in the numeration. For his Old Testament, Luther consulted primarily the Hebrew Bible printed at Brescia in 1494. Luther's copy of this book is now preserved in Berlin. Luther also consulted the Septuagint, the Vulgate, and the new Latin versions of Sanctes Pagninus and Sebastian Munster, and commentaries such as the *Glossa Ordinaria* and those of Nicolaus de Lyra. In his revised 1534 Bible, Luther was the first to separate the books of the Apocrypha from the body of the Old Testament.

Though it was not his intention, Luther became the Father of Protestantism. His theology challenged the authority of the papacy by holding that the Bible is the only infallible source of religious authority and that all baptized believers in Christ constitute a universal priesthood. Martin Luther believed that salvation is a free gift of God, received only by true repentance and faith in Jesus as the Messiah. Through his study of the Scriptures he understood that true faith is given by God, not mediated by the Church.

October 31, 1517 – Martin Luther & the 95 Theses

The "Matthew's" Bible

1537

The "Matthew's" Bible is John Roger's completion of the William Tyndale translation. This complete English Bible, welding together the best work of William Tyndale and improving upon the completion efforts of Miles Coverdale, is the true primary version of our English Bible, more so than the 1535 English Bible of Miles Coverdale.

John Rogers uses the pseudonym Thomas Matthew, not for himself, but for the martyred William Tyndale, because any association with William Tyndale was still outlawed. This Bible was able to be printed by "The King's Most Gracious License"—which would not have been granted to a "Tyndale" Bible. Yet, in tribute to Tyndale, John Rogers placed the large flourished initials "W.T." at the end of Malachi as a sign of Tyndale's authorship. It was his subtle message to the "secret society" underground of like-minded Reformers. (The second edition of the "Matthew's" Bible was printed during the brief reign of Edward VI in 1549 and openly contains the preface "William Tyndale Unto the Christian Reader.")

The "Matthew's" Bible

The First Edition of the Miles Coverdale "Great Bible"

1539

To Miles Coverdale goes the honor of the first complete Bible in English, his 1535 edition. That edition was not as fine a rendering as the 1537 "Matthew's" Bible which John Rogers saw through the press, because Rogers likely had more extensive access to William Tyndale's final manuscripts. Coverdale, ever servant to

God's Word, took it upon himself to improve even upon the "Matthew's" Bible, and in 1539 under the direct patronage of Thomas Cromwell, published the first edition of what is known as the "Great" Bible—one of the grandest and most beautiful Bibles ever produced. The second and subsequent editions of Coverdale's "Great" Bible are sometimes referred to as "Cranmer's" Bible because the Archbishop of Canterbury, Thomas Cranmer, contributed a Prologue to those versions. Miles Coverdale delivered a particularly mellifluous rendering of the Book of Psalms, and it is his version of the Psalter that has been generally maintained in the Bibles of the Church of England, and the various editions of the Book of Common Prayer.

Thomas Cranmer,
Archbishop of Canterbury

As the reign of King Henry VIII continued, the Bible in English was frequently reprinted. Under his son and successor, young Edward VI (reigned 1547-1553), the Bible in English continued to flourish, with some forty editions appearing. When Queen Mary ("Bloody Mary") took the throne in 1553, she determined to repress Scripture in English and once again the English Bible became a forbidden book. Among the first martyrs Queen Mary sent to the stake for heresy were John Rogers, the follower of William Tyndale who had published the 1537 "Matthew's" Bible, and Thomas Cranmer who had contributed the Prologue to the second and succeeding editions of Coverdale's "Great" Bible.

The "Geneva" Bible

1560

Under the Marian repressions, scholars of English Scripture and British theologians of the Reformation took refuge in Geneva, Switzerland under the protection of John Calvin. Although Queen Mary had John Rogers and Thomas Cranmer killed, Miles Coverdale was able to escape to Geneva.

The "Geneva" Bible of 1560 is *the* Bible of the English Reformation, and one of the most important books in the history of printing. It was the first English Bible with numbered verses. It was the Bible of the Puritans in England. It was the Bible of the Pilgrims, the first Bible brought to America, both to Virginia and

Massachusetts. It was the Bible through which John Smith witnessed to Pocahontas and her people. It was the Bible read and quoted by Shakespeare. William Shakespeare, often erroneously given credit for contributing to the King James Bible of 1611 was, in fact, steeped in the Geneva Bible that was first published four years before his birth and dominated the cultural landscape of Elizabethan England; he quotes from or clearly alludes to the Geneva translation hundreds of times in his Histories, Tragedies, and Comedies.

It was the Geneva Bible that held the hearts and souls of English-speaking believers in the Old World and the New for almost two hundred years. The Geneva translation was mostly the work of William Whittingham, a close associate of John Calvin in Switzerland, though, like all English Bibles, it was predominantly the Tyndale Bible in both spirit and wording. Whittingham had published his New Testament in 1557. His complete Bible of 1560 is the single most significant English printing of the Bible between the "Matthew's" Bible of 1537 and the King James Bible of 1611. William Whittingham was the first translator of the English Bible since Tyndale to have a thorough command of Hebrew, and thus the Geneva can be considered the first complete English Bible to be translated demonstrably from the original tongues of Hebrew and Greek.

1560 "Geneva" Bible opened to New Testament title page

John Calvin

The strong Calvinist marginal commentary of this Bible greatly endeared it to the radical Protestant movement, and caused equally great discomfort to the Church of England and the Church at Rome, who eventually responded with their "Bishops' Bible" and the "Rheims-Douai" Bible, respectively. The notes in the Geneva Bible grew even more radical in fresh campaigns of 1576 and 1602; it was mostly reprints of the radical 1602 "Geneva-Tomson-Junius" Bible that came to American shores.

The "Bishops' Bible"

1568

Under the reign of Queen Elizabeth, the printing of the English Bible was again permitted as it had been under Edward VI. The Church of England decided to react against the strong Calvinist tone of the 1560 "Geneva" Bible by publishing the pulpit folio "Bishops' Bible" in 1568, under the guidance of Bishop Matthew Parker. This Bible is generally considered one of the most elegant in presentation, but among the least elegant in translation *per se*. The "Bishops' Bible" was never able to capture the hearts and souls of English laypersons in the same manner as had the "Geneva" Bible.

Elizabeth I

The Cassiodoro de Reina Spanish Bible

1569

Cassiodoro de Reina was born in Seville in 1520 and grew up to be a Catholic monk there. However, influenced by Reformation writings, he became a Protestant and under pursuit by the Inquisition fled to Germany in 1557, then to England, then to The Netherlands. He worked constantly on his translation into Spanish from the Greek versions of Erasmus and the 1528 Latin edition of Sanctes Pagninus, as well as earlier New Testament work in Spanish by Francisco (sometimes Fransisco) de Enzinas and Juan Perez de Pineda. His Bible in Spanish was published in Basel, Switzerland in 1569. The Roman Church rejected and banned

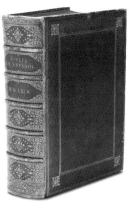

his Spanish vernacular edition of Scripture. De Reina was burned in effigy by the Inquisition but he escaped arrest under the protection of the Continental Reformers. He eventually settled in Frankfurt, where he organized an evangelical church and remained their pastor until his death in 1594. In 1602, a significant new edition of this Bible was published after twenty years of revision work by Cipriano de Valera. This Bible has henceforth been known as the Reina-Valera Bible, a cornerstone of Spanish Biblical translations, its latest revision being that of 1960.

*1569 Casiodoro de Reina
Bible in Spanish*

34

The Rheims New Testament

1582

By the time the "Geneva" Bible had become thoroughly adopted among readers of English, a scholarly group of Catholics at the English Roman Catholic College (in France, alternately at Rheims or Douai), undertook a specifically Catholic Englishing of Scripture. The work was accomplished by Gregory Martin, under the guidance of William Allen and Richard Bristow. This translation, by imperative and inclination, adheres more to the Latin Vulgate of Jerome than did the Tyndale and subsequent Reformation efforts, but Martin did confer with the Protestant Englishings and with "the Greeke and other editions in diverse languages" as stated on the title page. Despite his overly vitriolic prefatory attacks on Tyndale, Martin did, in fact, refer to Tyndale's versions, as well as the many others he consulted. The Catholic Englishing of the New Testament was first published in Rheims in 1582, and—although prepared by 1582—the Old Testament did not appear in print until 1609-1610, in two volumes published in Douai. Thus, this complete Bible is called the "Douai-Rheims" Bible. It is worth noting that this Catholic version of Scripture was Englished in advance of the 1592 revision of the Jerome Vulgate published under Pope Clementine VIII. In the mid-18th Century the Douai-Rheims Bible was thoroughly and painstakingly updated by Richard Challoner, and versions afterwards are sometimes referred to as the Douai-Rheims-Challoner Bible. [Douai is alternately spelled Douay.]

1582 Rheims New Testament

The King James Bible

1611

The King James Bible, also called the "Authorized Version," was conceived at the Hampton Court Conference of 1604, spent years in the making and revising, and was finally published in 1611. [Note 10] Upon the death of Elizabeth I in 1603, King James VI of Scotland became King James I of England. The council he convened (under Puritan pressure) at Hampton Court resolved "that a translation be made of the whole Bible, as consonant as can be to the original Hebrew and Greek; and this be set out and printed, without marginal notes, and only to be used in all churches of England in time of divine service." King James appointed 54 translators to the task (of whom 47 are known to have worked on the project), and thus the King James Bible is often referred to as the only great translation accomplished by a committee (certainly this is true when compared to the relative failure of the 1568 "Bishops' Bible"), though alterations in the text were not as significant when compared to earlier Englishings as was the simple act of deleting the marginal commentary of the Geneva Bible.

On exhibit are copies of all five printings of the first edition of the King James Bible, including the very first issue, known to bibliographers as the "Great He" Bible because of a misprint in Ruth 3:15, referring to Ruth as "he."

The first printing of the King James Version was a massive pulpit "folio" edition. By 1612, the new version was being printed in the smaller "quarto" size, intended to be handier for home use and private devotionals, and the exhibit shows some of these smaller versions, which were expressly intended, by both format and retail price, to supplant the Geneva Bibles for home use.

The King James Bible was not capable of immediately displacing the Geneva version in the hearts and souls of devout laypersons. It would be several generations before the Geneva version was eclipsed and the King James Version thoroughly adopted. But once the King James Bible was embraced, it held the hearts and souls of the faithful throughout the English-speaking world without challenge until the late 19th Century. The King James Bible remains one of the most-printed and most-loved books in the history of the world. To a great extent, this translation continues to show the hand—and the faith—of William Tyndale, whose solitary work is dominant throughout the King James Version and has never been excelled by subsequent translators, whether working alone or in committee.

1611 King James Bible

THE BIBLE IN AMERICA

The First Bible Printed in America

1663

The first Bible printed in America, dated 1663, was a missionary Bible in the Native America dialect of Algonquian. This Bible, officially titled *Mamusse Wunneetupanatamwe Up-Biblum God Naneeswe Nukkone Testament Kah Wonk Wusku Testament*, is more conveniently called "The Eliot Indian Bible" after its translator, the great and indefatigable American missionary John Eliot (dubbed by Cotton Mather as "The Apostle to the Indians"), one of the men responsible for the very first book printed in colonial America, the 1640 metrical Psalter titled *The Bay Psalm Book*. Eliot took very seriously the Massachusetts Bay Colony's original founding pledge to "wynne and incite the Natives to the knowledge and obedience of the only true Son and Saviour of Mankind and the Christian Fayth."

John Eliot was born in Nashing, Essex County, England in 1604 and studied for the Ministry at Cambridge University from 1618 to 1622. Because he aligned himself with the Puritan Nonconformists, he was precluded from preaching

John Eliot preaching to the Indians

in England. After the Anglican Church redoubled the persecution of the Nonconformists, John Eliot immigrated to these shores in 1631, just eleven years after the very first Pilgrims arrived on the *Mayflower*. He was twenty-seven years old and made the trans-Atlantic voyage with all his worldly goods: a few changes of clothes and twenty-three barrels of books. He quickly became the interim pastor of the First Church of Boston, but in 1632 settled in Roxbury and organized the First Church of Roxbury, where he pastored until his death in 1690. In 1644 Eliot took his first decisive step toward missionary commitment by enlisting the language instruction skills of a Native Algonquian named Cockanoe, born a Montauk and brought to Boston as a captive from the war against the Pequot. In 1654 John Eliot published his Algonquian versions of his *Indian Primer and Catechism*, and in

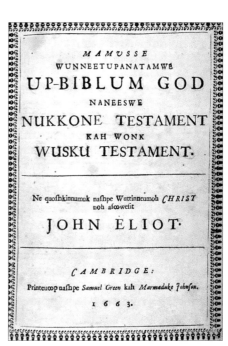

The Eliot Indian Bible,
title page

1658 his Algonquian *Book of Psalms* was published. When queried by local skeptics about why the Massachusetts Indians should have the Bible of the Jews and the Saints, John Eliot is said to have exclaimed: "The Bible is the Word of Life—they must have it!"

The Eliot Indian Bible is important for several reasons. It points out the fact that the Bible in English was often a forbidden book: it could not be printed legally by Colonial printers as such an act would be a violation of the "King's Copyright" on the text of the Bible—the King of England claiming copyright privilege on God's Word. Therefore, the first Bible printed in America was not in English but in Algonquian! The Eliot Bible is also important for its indication of the high missionary zeal of Colonial America. From the standpoint of Bible translations, and certainly speaking to the purpose of this exhibition, the Eliot Indian Bible represents a profound turning-point in the history of Scripture translation.

Since antiquity, the history of translation exemplified by the manuscripts and printed books in this exhibition is a history of translating scripture from an ancient or unfamiliar language into a more modern and more common one. With Eliot's Bible in Algonquian, the process began to go the other way, with the Bible in English being translated into an obscure indigenous language of the New World. This process of bringing Holy Scripture into native languages of the New World and the Third World is still in process.

The Saur Bible

1743

The first Bible printed in a European language in America is a Bible in German, printed by Christopher Saur in Germantown, Pennsylvania in 1743. Saur's Bible was the Luther version, a reprint of the 34th edition, with the books of III and IV Esdras and III Maccabees supplied from the Berlenberg Bible of 1726-42.

In Colonial America there were no copyright problems concerning Bibles in languages other than English. However, the Bible in English was then a forbidden book, with copyright rigidly controlled by the King of England.

The First English Language Bible Printed in America

1782

Upon our Declaration of Independence, the exportation of Bibles from Great Britain to the rebelling Colonies was heavily curtailed. Our Revolution enabled us to break royal copyright control on the text of the King James Bible. In 1782 the first Bible printed in English in America was published in Philadelphia by Robert Aitken, the official printer to the United States Congress—in direct and deliberate violation of King's copyright and in defiant answer to the Bible embargo. This Bible became known as "The Bible of the Revolution."

The 1782 Aitken Bible was initiated by an unprecedented Congressional Resolution regarding "Aitken's impression of the Holy Scriptures of the Old and New Testament." It reads as follows:

"Sept 10th, 1782:

'Whereupon, RESOLVED, that the United States in Congress Assembled highly approve the pious and laudable undertaking of Mr. Aitken, as subservient to the interest of religion, as well as an instance of the progress of arts in this country…, *they recommend this edition of the Bible to the inhabitants of the United States.*'"

This Resolution of Congress, and their direct involvement in the domestic spread of Scripture, should allay any doubts as to where our Founding Fathers stood in relation to their God. (As should a re-reading of George Washington's First Inaugural Address.)

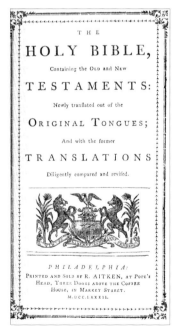

The Bible of the Revolution

Once freed from royal restraint, the King James Bible flourished in America, with Congress imposing no copyright on the existing translations. In order to comply with the varying sentiments regarding the inclusion of the Apocrypha and marginal commentary, Isaac Collins, in his famous family Bible of 1791 provided subscribers to this edition the choice of including or excluding them in their personal copies. In the preface to his Bible, Isaac Collins boldly wrote: "As the Dedication of the English translation of the Bible to King James the First of England seems to be wholly unnecessary for the purposes of edification, and perhaps on some accounts improper to be continued in an American edition, the Editor has been advised by some judicious friends to omit it."

By 1800 there were already seventy printings of the King James Bible by American printers, and by 1840 over a thousand. The first Bible for Catholics printed in the United States was in Philadelphia in 1790 in the Douai-Rheims-Challoner version. The American "Family Bible"—large and usually extensively illustrated—became a fixture in the 19th and 20th Century American home.

The first Bible printed in America by a woman was the 1808 Thomson Septuagint in English printed by Jane Aitken, daughter of Robert Aitken.

For further evidence of the religious faith of our Founding Fathers, note the example below of a letter written by Thomas Jefferson. In this letter, Jefferson expresses most firmly his belief in a God who is active in our world. Referring to the patriots of Holland, in their struggle against the ruling House of Orange, Jefferson writes to a friend, Mr. Tench Coxe, regarding the recent victories of the armed patriot militias of the Dutch Republic: *"I congratulate you on the successes of our two allies. Those of the Hollanders are new, and therefore pleasing. It proves there is a God in Heaven, and that He will not slumber without end on the iniquities of tyrants, or would-be tyrants, as their Stadtholder* [referring to Willem the Fifth of the House of Orange]. *This ball of liberty, I believe most piously, is now so well in motion that it will roll round the globe, at least the enlightened part of it, for light & liberty go together. It is our glory that we first put it into motion, & our happiness that being foremost we had no bad examples to follow..."*

Thomas Jefferson, writing from Monticello in 1795

The Lunar Bible

1971

Several microfilm copies of the King James Bible went to the Moon with Lunar Module Pilot Edgar Mitchell on the mission of *Apollo 14*, arriving on the lunar surface on February 5, 1971, marking the first time that Holy Scripture left our planet. This Bible was produced by the Apollo Prayer League of Houston, a group of NASA engineers, scientists, administrators, and astronauts under the direction of Rev. John Stout, Senior Information Scientist of the Apollo Program. Measuring only 2x2 inches and containing 1,245 tiny pages, this microfilm includes the full text of the King James Bible.

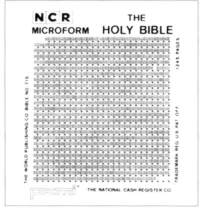

The microfilm Lunar Bible

Postscript

We have chosen to end the translation history of this exhibition with the King James Version for historical and practical reasons, not theological ones. The early Bibles in English printed in the United States were all the King James Version, and these were printed without copyright. This version of the Bible held the field unchallenged until the late 19th Century. In the 20th Century a proliferation of new English translations were published (and continue to be published), leaving theologians with much to debate, publishers with many new copyrights on the Word of God, and would-be purchasers of new Bibles with much to be confused about. It has not been the purpose of this exhibition to endorse one translation over another, though, clearly, we have a profound respect and appreciation for the continuing value of the work of William Tyndale, whose work permeates every English Bible from 1526 until this century. It has certainly not been the purpose of this exhibition to espouse a specific Christian theology. Rather, we have hoped to instill through this exhibition a new respect for all the men and women of faith who have worked tirelessly and suffered greatly to take bold stands and serious risks to shape the English Bible for us. We hope that through this experience we will never again take our personal or family Bibles for granted. We further, and most importantly, hope that learning more about this dramatic history of Holy Scripture will lead us to a more profound reading of God's Word itself.

omnes partincipes eius rotundentur.
Fabri enim sunt ex hominibs. Conue=
nient omnes:stabūt ⁊ pauebūt:⁊ con=
fundent simul. Faber ferrarius lima o=
peratus est:in prunis ⁊ in malleis for=
mauit illud:et operatus est in brachi=
o fortitudinis sue. Esuriet et deficiet:
non bibet aquā et lassescet. Artifex li=
gnariꝰ extēdit normā:formauit illud
in runcina. Fecit illud ī angularibs:
et ī circino tornauit illud:et fecit yma=
ginem uiri quasi speciosum hominē
habitātem in domo. Succidit cedros:
tulit ilicem et quercū que steterat inter
ligna saltus. Plātauit pinū quā plu=
uia nutriuit:et facta est hominibs in
focū. Sumpsit ex eis et calefactus est:
et succendit et coxit panes:de reliquo
autē operarꝰ est deū et adorauit:fecit
sculptile·et curuatꝰ est ante illud. Me=
dium eius combussit igni : de medio
eius carnes coxit. Comedit pulmentū
et saturatus ē:et calefactus est ⁊ dixit.
Vah calefactꝰ sum:uidi focū. Reliquū
autē eius·deū fecit ⁊ sculptile sibi. Cur=
uatur ante illud:et adorat illud ⁊ ob=
secrat dicens. libera me:quia deus me=
us es tu. Nescierūt neq; intellexerunt.
Obliti enim sunt ne uideāt oculi eoꝝ:
et ne intelligant corde suo. Non reco=
gitant in mente sua:neq; cognoscunt
neq; sentiūt ut dicant. Medietatē eiꝰ
combussi igni : et coxi sup carbones e=
ius panes. Coxi carnes et comedi : et
de reliquo eius ydolum faciā? Ante
truncū ligni pridam? Pars eiꝰ cinis
est. Cor insipiens adorauit illud:et
non liberauit animā suā : neq; dicit

mei. Deleui ut nube iniquitates tu
et quasi nebulā peccata tua. Reuerte
ad me : quoniā redemi te. laudate
quoniā misericordiā fecit dūs:iub
te extrema terre. Resonate montes l
dationem:saltus et omne lignū ei
Quoniā redemit dūs iacob:et isra
gloriabitur. Hec dicit dūs redemp
tuus:⁊ formator tuus ex utero. Ego
minus faciens omnia:extendens c
solus. Stabiliens terrā et nullus
cū:irrita faciēs signa diuinoꝝ:⁊ a
los ī furorē vertens. Cōuertēs sapi
retroꝛsū: et scientiā eoꝛ stultā facie
Suscitās verbū serui sui : et cons
nūcioꝛ suoꝛ cōplēs. Qui dico ihr
habitaberis : et ciuitatibus iuda
ficabimini : et deserta eius suscita
Qui dico profundo desolare : et
mina tua arefaciam. Qui dico r
pastoꝛ meꝰ es : et omnē volūtatē n
complebis. Qui dico iherusalem
ficaberis:et tēplo fūdaberis. XL
Hec dicit dūs cristo meo cyro c
apphendi dexteram ut subici
ante faciem eius gentes : et dorsa
gum vertā. Et aperiā corā eo ianu
et porte nō claudentur. Ego ante
bo:⁊ gloriosos terre humiliabo. P
tas ereas cōteram:⁊ vectes ferreos c
fringā. Et dabo tibi thesauros absc
ditos et archana secretoꝛ:ut scias
ego dūs · ꝗ voco nomē tuū deus ī
hel : propter seruū meū iacob ⁊ isra
electū meū. Et vocaui te noīe tuo
similaui te:et nō cognouisti me.
domin9:et non est āplius. Extra
non est deus. Accinxi te et nō cog

APPENDIX

Notes on the Canon(s) of Scripture and The Apocrypha

The issues of the Canon of Scripture, especially relating to what Protestant denominations call The Apocrypha and what Roman Catholics call the Deuterocanonical Books, are complex and deserving of more detailed attention than I can give them here, but I hope this will constitute an acceptable introduction to the subject, with a balanced guide of suggestions for further reading.

The Apocrypha is a collection of Jewish works from approximately 300 B.C. to the First Century A.D.—also known collectively as the "intertestamental books" by modern Christians—which are not included in the Hebrew Bible but are accepted as canonical, that is to say, as authoritative Scripture, by some Christians. These books were composed in Hebrew, Greek, and Aramaic.

The Canon of Scripture varies from the Tanakh (Hebrew Bible) to the Catholic Old Testament to the Protestant Old Testament. These differences hinge on fourteen specific books from the intertestamental period known to Protestants as The Apocrypha. These fourteen books were placed between the Old and New Testaments in all early Protestant Bibles in English from the Coverdale Bible of 1535 to the King James Bible ("Authorized Version") of 1611. The King James Bible continued to include The Apocrypha until the Archbishop of Canterbury removed it from Holy Scripture for the Anglican Church (Church of England) in 1885. The British & Foreign Bible Society (formed 1809) had dropped The Apocrypha from their printings of the Bible in 1826.

These fourteen books had long been considered as non-inspired by certain Protestant denominations, e.g. The Puritans, who would sometimes physically remove The Apocrypha from their copies of the Bible, even their especially beloved Geneva Bibles. Statements of the non-inspired status of the Apocrypha are as early as the Calvinist "Gallic Confession" (1559) and the "Belgic Confession" (1561) and the proclamations of the Synod of Dort (1619). The Westminster Confession (1646) for the Presbyterians includes: "The books commonly called the Apocrypha, not being of divine inspiration, are no part of the canon of the Scripture; and therefore are of no authority in the Church of God, nor to be in any otherwise approved, or made use of, than other human writings." Several immediately subsequent Baptist Confessions of Faith were equal in their opinions. John Calvin was forthright in his rejection of the books of the Apocrypha from canonical consideration for the newly emerging Protestant Reformation faiths, though he was very well read in them and respected them in the same manner as the Westminster Confession, and, as anyone visiting this exhibition can see, the

Left: Gutenberg Bible page

43

"Geneva" Bible contained The Apocrypha. The Introduction to that section clarifies the Calvinistic stance on the subject just one year after the "Gallic Confession" and is deserving of being quoted here in its entirety (with the original spellings):

> *"These bokes that follow in order after the Prophets unto the Newe Testament are called Apocrypha, that is bokes which were not received by a comune consent to be red and expounded publickely in the Church, neither yet served to prove any point of Christian religion save in asmuche as they had the consent of the other Scriptures called Canonical to confirme the same, or rather whereon they were grounded: but as bokes proceding from godlie men, were received to be red for the advancement and furtherance of the knowledge of the historie, and for the instruction of godlie manners: which bokes declare that at all times God had an especial care of his Church and left them not utterly destitute of teachers and means to confirme them in the hope of the promised Messiah, and also witnesse that those calamities that God sent to his Church, were according to his providence who had bothe so threatened by his Prophets, and so brought it to passe for the destruction of their enemies, and for the tryal of his children."*

John Wyclif and Martin Luther thought (as did Saint Jerome) that the books of the Apocrypha should be utilized as edifying literature, in the sense of any good devotional classic (one thinks of *The Imitation of Christ* by Thomas a Kempis or *The Pilgrim's Progress* by John Bunyan). The books of the Apocrypha are in the Wycliffite manuscripts of the Old Testament just as expected in the Catholic order and placement, and are in the Luther Bibles (extracted from the Old Testament for the first time in print and placed between the Testaments, as became the norm of the Reformation Bibles).

When speaking of any books that may have been considered as Scripture by one group or another, but were never "canonized" by the Roman or Eastern Churches or a Protestant denomination, one should use the terms apocryphal books (with a lower case "a") or pseudepigrapha where that technical term is appropriate. These terms denote an ill-defined body of material outside of Scripture which contains books such as: [Old Testament Period] Enoch, Jubilees, 2 Baruch, Book of Jasher, Testaments of the Twelve Patriarchs; [New Testament Period] Didache, Gospel of Thomas, Shepherd of Hermas, etc.

For the doctrinal stance of one's own church or denomination, one should inquire of one's Pastor, Preacher, Priest or Rabbi. For an overall historical view, one should do some reading in all three perspectives: Jewish, Catholic and Protestant.

NOTES

Note 1

The Leningrad Codex, or *Codex Leningradensis*, is the oldest complete Hebrew Bible known to exist. While there are older portions of Bibles (notably the *Aleppo Codex*), or scriptural books, there is no older manuscript which contains the whole Hebrew Bible, or Tanakh. This manuscript was written around 1005–1010 A.D. It is called the *Codex Leningradensis* because it resides at the Russian National Library (Saltykov-Shchedrin) in St. Petersburg (formerly Leningrad) where it has been since the mid-1800s. This manuscript is the oldest known of a group of Hebrew texts called the Masoretic texts, after a group called the Masoretes who were especially concerned with the accurate transmission of texts of Scripture from the early Medieval period forward.

Note 2

These seven manuscripts now form the core collection of the Israeli "Shrine of the Book" museum in Jerusalem. They are Isaiah A (1QisaA), Isaiah B (1Q8), the War Scroll (1QM), Hodayot A (1QH), Pesher Habakkuk (1QpHab), the Genesis Apocryphon (1Qap-Gen), and the Rule of the Community (1QS). After the 1967 Arab-Israeli War, the Temple Scroll (11Q19) was added to the collection. The Shrine of the Book now has other findings, material culture, Bar-Kokhba material and the Aleppo Codex.

Note 3

For modern usage the recommended editions of the Septuagint are the third edition (1949) edited by Alfred Rahlfs and published by the Wurttemberg Bible Society or the Gottingen Septuagint published by Joseph Ziegler in 1965.

Note 4

This document, commonly though erroneously called the "Edict of Milan," may be found in divergent forms in Eusebius (*Hist. Eccl.*, x. 5) (see also his *Vita Constantini*) and Lactantius (*De Mortibus Persecutorum*, xlviii).

Note 5

The great Christian scholar Origen lived about 186-254 A.D. Circa 230-245 A.D. he completed his most famous work, the imposing Hexapla, one of the greatest achievements in textual criticism of the period. This massive work compared and contrasted the Hebrew text of his day with a Greek transliteration, a revision of the Septuagint, and the post-Septuagint Greek translations of Aquila (from circa 130 A.D.), Theodotion (also 2nd Century A.D.), and Symmachus (slightly later, probably 3rd Century A.D.). Regrettably, there are no extant manuscripts of the Hexapla.

Note 6

The earliest extant manuscript of the Jerome Vulgate is the *Codex Amiatinus*, produced in the twin monasteries of Jarrow and Monkwearmouth some time before 716 A.D., and now at the Biblioteca Medicea Laurenziana in Florence. The recommended modern Latin edition of the Bible is the *Biblia Sacra* edited by Robert Weber, the revised edition of 1971 published in Stuttgart.

Note 7

Among Catholics and Protestants alike, the Latin Bible received a great deal of attention during the 16th Century as a result of the Reformation and Counter-Reformation. The first "critical" edition of the Vulgate text was printed by Robert Estienne (sometimes Stephanus) in 1528 and was revised for a second edition in 1532. 1528 also saw the Latin Bible of the Dominican Sanctes Pagninus. Sebastian Munster's Latin version reached print in 1534/35, and Leo Juda's in 1544. In 1546, the key year of the Council of Trent, the Catholic Church decreed the Vulgate as irreproachable inspired Holy Scripture, finalizing the Vatican's stance on the Catholic Canon. The Vatican-authorized Sixtus/Clementine recension was published in 1590/92 and remained the definitive Bible for the Catholic Church.

Note 8

Legal restrictions on the Bible in English began with the Act of 1401 called *De Haeretico Comburendo* ("that heretics should be burned") and took full effect with Arundel's Constitutions of 1409. [*De Haeretico Comburendo* [2 Henry IV. cap. 15: *Statutes of the Realm*, ii, 125.] This act specifically calls for Lollards (followers of the doctrines of John Wyclif) to be burned at the stake in public "that such punishment may strike fear into the minds of others." This Act was expanded under Henry V, repealed late in the reign of Henry VIII, revived under Queen Mary, and repealed permanently under Elizabeth I.

Note 9

The Wycliffite Manuscript shown in the photograph is a genuine martyr's Bible which once belonged to Richard Hunne. Richard Hunne was a most dedicated servant of God and Scripture. He deliberately put himself in harm's way many times in his belief in Scripture in English and his disapproval of the canon laws of the Church. He was known to read aloud to passersby from this Wycliffite Bible or his other Wycliffite Bible (now at Corpus Christi College, Cambridge). In 1511, Hunne refused to pay a mortuary fee to the priest who said the funeral mass for his 5-week-old son. Under canon law, a mortuary fee was due to the priest who performed the funeral service, and the fee was expressed to be any possession of the deceased requested by the priest. In this case, the priest requested only the cloth used to wrap the baby, but Hunne refused, citing civil law that a 5-week-old baby could not, under English law, be considered the owner of anything. Hunne wished the case to go to civil court, but it went to Spiritual Court at Lambeth. The charge was heresy, as any violation of canon law could bring such a charge. While this case was not yet publicly adjudicated, Hunne attended a Mass and was asked by the presiding priest to leave the Mass, as he would not continue with a heretic in the Church. Again deliberately putting himself in severe jeopardy, Hunne took legal action: he sued this presiding priest for slander, claiming that he was slandered by the priest's having called him a heretic in public when that case had not yet been determined. Hunne invoked the Great Statute of Praemunire in these suits. This statute of Praemunire had been enacted into the English Law Code in 1393 by Richard II and simply stated that there was no higher authority in England than the King of England. But, under these circumstances, the case was not so simple. If a panel of judges were to concede the validity of this statute in this case, they would have to rule against canon law in a Spiritual Court, thus subjecting themselves to possible charges of heresy. On the other hand, if they were to place canon law above the Great Statute of Praemunire, they would be, *de jure*, guilty of treason against their King. This insoluble dilemma led those authorities involved to decide that the best way out was to murder Richard Hunne. A young Henry VIII was watching these Hunne suits very closely, and Hunne's setting of the two conflicting legal systems on a collision course steeled the King for future open conflicts with Rome. It is interesting to continue the ownership trail of Hunne's Bible, as it went by descent to his daughter Alice Hunne, and then by marriage into the Winthrop family, which eventually came to settle the Massachusetts Bay Colony. In the 19th Century this Wycliffite Bible became the property of Mary Baker Eddy, author of *Science and Health, with a Key to the Scriptures*, the cornerstone work of Christian Science.

Note 10

The King James Bible was never actually "authorized" by the King, but common usage of the phrase has led to this translation often being referred to as the Authorized Version, or AV, especially in England.

Herfoze, seyng that we haue suche an offyce, euen as mercy is come on vs, *we faynte not: but haue caste from vs the clokes of vnhonestie, and walke not in craftynes, nether a*handle we the wozde of God disceitfullye: but in open truth, and repozte oure selues to euery mannes conscience in the syght of God. If oure Gospell be yet hyd, it is hyd amonge them that are lost, in whom the God of this wozlde hathe blynded the mindes of them whiche beleue not, lest the light of the glozious Gospell of Christ which is the ymage of God, should shyne vnto them.

B Foz we pzeache not our selues, but Christ Jesus to be the Lozd, and oure selues youre seruauntes, foz Jesus sake. Foz it is God that commaunded the lyght to shyne out of darcknes, which hath shyned in oure hertes, foz to geue the lyght of the knowledge of the glozy of God, in the face of Jesus Christe.

But we haue this b*treasure in erthen vessels, that the excellencye of the power, myghte be Goddes and not oures. We are troubled on euery syde, yet are we not without shift. We are in pouerty: but not vtterly without somwhat. We are persecuted: but are not fozsaken. We are cast doune: neuerthelesse we perishe not. And we alwayes beare aboute in our bodye, the dyinge of the L O R D E Jesus, that the lyfe of Jesu myght also appere in oure bodyes.

Foz we which lyue are alwayes deliuered vnto death foz Jesus sake, that the lyfe also of Jesu myght appere in oure moztal flesshe. So then death wozketh in vs, and life in you. Seynge then that we haue the same spzite of fayth, accozdynge as it is wzitten: J beleued, and therfoze haue J spoken. We also beleue, ⁊ therfoze speake. Foz we knowe that he which raysed vp the Lozde Jesus, shall rayse vp vs also by the meanes of Jesus, and shall set vs with you. Foz all thynges do J foz youre sakes that the plenteous grace by thanckes geuen of many, maye redounde to the pzayse of God.

Wherfoze, we are not weried, but though oure vtwarde

SUGGESTIONS FOR FURTHER READING
ON THE HISTORY OF THE BIBLE

(These are recommended entry-level works for further study. Please see our following alphabetical Bibliography for more advanced works in each area.)

GENERAL BIBLE HISTORY AND THE BIBLE IN ENGLISH:

The Forbidden Book. By Dr. Craig Lampe. (Goodyear, AZ: The Bible Museum, 2003.

The Book. A History of the Bible. By Christopher de Hamel. (London and New York: Phaidon Press, 2001) A superb introductory text of the history of the Bible.

The Origin of the Bible. Edited by Philip Wesley Comfort. (Wheaton, Illinois: Tyndale House Publishers, 1992)

The Bible in English. Its History and Influence. By Dr. David Daniell. (Yale University Press [UK edition], 2003). The definitive book on the topic by a leading scholar in the field.

William Tyndale: A Biography. By Dr. David Daniell. (New Haven, Connecticut: Yale University Press, 2001 [paperback edition of Yale Nota Bene])

Wide as the Waters. The Story of the English Bible and the Revolution It Inspired. By Benson Bobrick. (New York: Simon & Schuster, 2001)

The Journey from Texts to Translations. The Origin and Development of the Bible. By Paul D. Wegner. (Grand Rapids: Baker Academic, 1999)

THE DEAD SEA SCROLLS:

The Complete World of the Dead Sea Scrolls. By Philip Davies, George Brooke and Phillip Callaway. (London and New York: Thames & Hudson, 2002) Superb comprehensive introductory overview, heavily illustrated.

The Dead Sea Scrolls Today. By James Vanderkam. (Grand Rapids: Eerdsmans, 1994)

Secrets of the Dead Sea Scrolls. By Randall Price. (Eugene, OR: Harvest House, 1996)

THE FORMATION OF THE HEBREW BIBLE (TANAKH):

The Jewish Study Bible. Adele Berlin and Marc Ziv Brettler, editors. Michael Fishbane, consulting editor. Jewish Publication Society TANAKH Translation. Oxford: Oxford University Press, 1999.

Surpassing Wonder. The Invention of The Bible and the Talmuds. By Donald Akenson. (Chicago: University of Chicago Press, 2001 [paperback edition]) A thorough look at the formation of the Hebrew Bible, the Mishnah, and the Talmuds. Lengthy, but the subject requires it. Not overly technical and certainly understandable by a newcomer to the subject.

The Septuagint (LXX):

Invitation to the Septuagint. By Karen Jobes and Moises Silva. (Grand Rapids, Michigan: Baker Academic, 2001) Accessible introduction to a very complex subject, one that is difficult to express any more simply than is done here.

The Development of the King James Bible:

In the Beginning. The Story of the King James Bible and How it Changed a Nation, a Language, and a Culture. By Alister McGrath. (New York: Doubleday, 2001)

God's Secretaries. The Making of the King James Bible. By Adam Nicholson. (New York: HarperCollins, 2003)

The Apocrypha:

Introducing the Apocrypha. Message–Context–Significance. By David A. deSilva. (Grand Rapids: Baker, 2002.)

The Parallel Apocrypha. John R. Kohlenberger III. Greek Text. King James Version. Douay Old Testament. The Holy Bible by Ronald Knox. Today's English Version. New Revised Standard Version. New American Bible. New Jerusalem Bible. New York & Oxford: Oxford University Press, 1997. Highly recommended also for its multiple perspective introductions covering the views of Jews, Catholics, Protestants, Anglicans, and Evangelicals.

BIBLIOGRAPHY

AKENSON, Donald Harman. *Surpassing Wonder. The Invention of the Bible and the Talmuds.* 1998.

ALAND, Kurt and Barbara. *The Text of the New Testament.* (trans. E. F. Rhodes) Second Edition, 1989.

ALAND, Kurt. Kurzgefasste *Liste der griechischen Handschriften des Neuen Testaments.* 1963.

BETTENSON, Henry and MAUNDER, Chris. *Documents of the Christian Church.* Third Edition, 1999.

BIENKOWSKI, Piotr and MILLARD, Alan (eds.) *Dictionary of the Ancient Near East.* 2000.

BOER, Harry R. *A Short History of the Early Church.* 1976. (reprint 1998).

BOURNE, Russell. *Gods of War, Gods of Peace. How the Meeting of Native and Colonial Religions Shaped Early America.* 2002.

BREMER, Francis J. *John Winthrop: America's Forgotten Founding Father.* 2003.

BRUCE, F. F. *The English Bible. A History of Translation.* 1961.

CAMPBELL, Jonathan G. *Dead Sea Scrolls. The Complete Story.* 1998.

CARTER, John, and MUIR, Percy. *Printing and the Mind of Man.* (Second edition, revised and enlarged, 1983)

CAVALLO, G. *Ricerche sulla maiuscola biblica.* (Studi e testi di papirologia, ii) 1967.

CLARK, K. W. *A Descriptive Catalogue of Greek New Testament Manuscripts in America.* 1939.

COGLEY, Richard. *John Eliot's Mission to the Indians before King Philip's War.* 1999.

COMFORT, Philip Wesley (ed.) *The Origin of the Bible.* 1992.

COULMAS, Florian. *The Writing Systems of the World.* 1991.

COULMAS, Florian (ed.). *The Blackwell Encyclopedia of Writing Systems.* 1999.

COULMAS, Florian. *Writing Systems. An Introduction to Their Linguistic Analysis.* 2003.

CHRISTIN, Anne-Marie. *A History of Writing. From Hieroglyph to Multimedia.* (English, 2002).

CROSS, F. L. (editor). *The Oxford Dictionary of the Christian Church.* Revised Second Edition, 1974.

DANIELL, David. *William Tyndale: A Biography.* 1994.

DANIELS, Peter T., and BRIGHT, William. *The World's Writing Systems.* 1996.

DARLOW, T. H. and MOULE, H. F. *Historical Catalogue of the Printed Editions of Holy Scripture in the Library of The British and Foreign Bible Society.* London, 1903-1911.

DAVIES, Philip R., BROOKE, George J. and CALLAWAY, Phillip R. *The Complete World of the Dead Sea Scrolls.* 2002.

DE HAMEL, Christopher. *The Book. A History of the Bible.* 2001.

DE HAMEL, Christopher. *A History of Illuminated Manuscripts.* (Second edition, revised and enlarged, 1994)

DeSILVA, David A. *Introducing the Apocrypha. Message–Context–Significance.* 2002.

DIRINGER, David. *The Alphabet. A Key to the History of Mankind.* Second and Revised Edition. 1948.

DIRINGER, David. *The Book Before Printing. Ancient, Medieval and Oriental.* (Dover reprint 1982; originally published in 1953 as *The Hand-Produced Book.*)

DOUGLAS, J.D. (general editor). *The New International Dictionary of the Christian Church.*

EHRMAN, Bart D. The New Testament. *A Historical Introduction to the Early Christian Writings.* 2000.

ELLIOTT, J. K. *A Survey of Manuscripts Used in Editions of the Greek New Testament.* 1987.

FRANCIS, Convers. *Life of John Eliot, the Apostle to the Indians.* 1836.

GOFF, Matthew. *"Wisdom, Apocalypticism, and the Pedagogical Ethos of 4QInstruction"* (Ph.D. thesis, Georgia Southern University, 2002)

GOODSPEED, Edgar J. *The Making of the English New Testament.* 1925.

GRANT, Frederick C. *Translating the Bible.* 1961.

GRENFELL, B. P. and HUNT, A. S. *The Oxyrynchus Papyri,* XI. 1915.

GRENFELL, B. P. and HUNT, A. S. *The Oxyrynchus Papyri*, XV. 1922.

HAINES-EITZEN, Kim. *Guardians of Letters. Literacy, Power and the Transmitters of Early Christian Literature.* 2000.

HEALEY, John F. *The Early Alphabet* (Reading the Past, Volume 9). 1991.

HERBERT, A. S. *Historical Catalogue of Printed Editions of the English Bible 1525-1961.* Revised and Expanded from the Edition of T. H. Darlow and H. F. Moule, 1903. 1968.

HILL, Christopher. *The English Bible and the Seventeenth-Century Revolution.* 1993.

HILLS, Margaret T. *The English Bible in America. A Bibliography of Editions of the Bible and the New Testament Published in America 1777-1957.* 1961.

JEAN, Georges. Writing. *The Story of Alphabets and Scripts.* 1992.

JOBES, Karen H. and SILVA, Moises. *Invitation to the Septuagint.* 2000.

KELLEY, Page, MYNATT, Daniel and CRAWFORD, Timothy. *The Masorah of the Biblia Hebraica Stuttgartensia.* 1998.

KILGOUR, Frederick G. *The Evolution of the Book.* 1998.

LAMPE, Craig H. *The Forbidden Book* (revised). 2003.

MacCULLOCH, Diarmaid. *The Reformation.* 2004 (U.S. edition).

MAGNESS, Jodi. *The Archaeology of Qumran and the Dead Sea Scrolls.* 2002.

MAN, John. *Gutenberg: How One Man Remade the World with Words.* 2002.

MARTIN, Henri-Jean. *The History and Power of Writing.* 1995.

McDONALD, Lee Martin, and SANDERS, James A. (General Editors). *The Canon Debate.* 2002.

McFARLANE, K.B. *John Wycliffe and the Beginnings of English Nonconformity.* 1953.

METZGER, Bruce M. *The Text of the New Testament. Its Transmission, Corruption, and Restoration.* 1992 (Third Edition).

METZGER, Bruce M. *The Bible in Translation. Ancient and English Versions.* 2001.

NAKANISHI, Akira. *Writing Systems of the World: Alphabets, Syllabaries, Pictograms.* 1990.

NICHOLSON, Adam. *God's Secretaries. The Making of the King James Bible.* 2003.

NISSEN, Hans, DAMEROW, Peter and ENGLUND, Robert. *Archaic Bookkeeping: Writing and Techniques of Economic Administration in the Ancient Near East.* 1993.

O'CALLAGHAN, Edmund Bailey. *A List of Editions of the Holy Scriptures and Parts Thereof Printed in America Previous to 1860.* 1861.

PESTMAN, P. W. *The New Papyrological Primer.* Second Edition, 1994.

PHILLIPS, Kevin. *The Cousins' Wars. Religion, Politics, and the Triumph of Anglo-America.* 1999.

POLLARD, Alfred W. *Records of the English Bible. The Documents Relating to the Translation and Publication of the Bible in English, 1525-1611.* 1911.

ROBINSON, Andrew. *The Story of Writing: Alphabets, Hieroglyphs and Pictograms.* 1999.

RUMBALL-PETRE, Edwin A. R. *Rare Bibles. An Introduction for Collectors and a Descriptive Checklist.* 1954.

SAMPSON, Geoffrey. *Writing Systems. A Linguistic Introduction.* 1990 re-issue.

SCHIFFMAN, Lawrence H. and VANDERKAM, James C. (eds.). *The Encyclopedia of the Dead Sea Scrolls.* Two volumes. 2000.

SCOTT, William, and RUGER, Hans Peter. *A Simplified Guide to Biblia Hebraica Stuttgartensia: Critical Apparatus, Masora, Accents, Unusual Letters and Other Markings.* 1995 (3/e).

SENNER, Wayne (ed.). *The Origins of Writing.* 1991 (reprint).

SHARPE, John L. and VAN KAMPEN, Kimberly. *The Bible as Book. The Manuscript Tradition.* 1998.

STEGEMANN, Hartmut. *The Library of Qumran.* 1993 (English 1998).

TIGCHELAAR, Elbert J. C. *To Increase Learning for the Understanding Ones. Reading and Reconstructing the Fragmentary Early Jewish Sapiential Text 4QInstruction.* 2001.

TOV, Emmanuel. *Textual Criticism of the Hebrew Bible.* Second edition, 2001.

TURNER, Eric G. *The Papyrologist at Work.* 1973.

VANDERKAM, James C. *The Dead Sea Scrolls Today.* 1994.

VAN HAELST, J. *Catalogue des papyrus litteraires juifs et chretiens.* 1976.

VERMES, Geza. *An Introduction to the Complete Dead Sea Scrolls.* 1999.

WALKER, C. B. F., *Cuneiform. (Reading the Past,* Volume 3). 1989.

WAQUET, Francoise. *Latin. Or the Empire of a Sign.* (translated by John Howe). 1998 (2001).

WEGNER, Paul D. *The Journey from Texts to Translations. The Origin and Development of the Bible.* 1999.

WURTHWEIN, Ernst. *The Text of the Old Testament. An Introduction to the Biblia Hebraica.* (trans. E. F. Rhodes) Second edition, 1995.

10 Iesus answered, & said vnto him, Art thou a master of Israel, and knowest not these things?

11 Verely, verely I say vnto thee, We speake that we do know, and testifie that we haue seen; and ye receiue not our witnesse.

12 If I haue told you earthly things, and ye beleeue not: how shall ye beleeue if I tell you of heauenly things?

13 And no man hath ascended vp to heauen, but he that came downe from heauen, euen the Sonne of man which is in heauen.

14 ¶ *And as Moses lifted vp the serpent in the wildernesse: euen so must the Sonne of man be lifted vp:

15 That whosoeuer beleeueth in him should not perish, but haue eternall life.

16 ¶ *For God so loued the world, that hee gaue his onely begotten Sonne: that whosoeuer beleeueth in him, should not perish, but haue euerlasting life.

17 *For God sent not his Sonne into the world to condemne the world: but that the world through him might be saued.

18 ¶ Hee that beleeueth on him, is not condemned: but he that beleeueth not, is condemned already, because hee hath not beleeued in the Name of the onely begotten Sonne of God.

19 And this is the condemnation, *that light is come into the world, and men loued darkenes rather then light, because their deeds were euill.

20 For euery one that doth euill, hateth the light, neither commeth to the light, lest his deeds should be ||reprooued.

21 But he that doth trueth, commeth to the light, that his deeds may be made manifest, that they are wrought in God.

22 ¶ After these things, came Iesus and his disciples into the land of Iudea, and there hee taried with them, * and baptized.

23 ¶ And Iohn also was baptizing in Aenon, neere to Salim, because there was much water there: and they came, and were baptized.

24 For Iohn was not yet cast into prison.

25 ¶ Then there arose a question betweene some of Iohns disciples and the Iewes, about purifying.

26 And they came vnto Iohn, and said vnto him, Rabbi, he that was with thee beyond Iordane, *to whom thou barest witnesse, behold, the same baptizeth, and all men come to him.

27 Iohn answered, & said, *A man can ||receiue nothing, except it be giuen him from heauen.

28 Ye your selues beare mee witnesse, that I said, *I am not the Christ, but that I am sent before him.

29 He that hath the bride, is the bridegrome: but the friend of the bridegrome, which standeth and heareth him, reioiceth greatly because of the bridegromes voyce: This my ioy therefore is fulfilled.

30 He must increase, but I must decrease.

31 He that commeth from aboue, is aboue all: he that is of the earth, is earthly, and speaketh of the earth: he that commeth from heauen is aboue all.

32 And what he hath seene and heard, that he testifieth, and no man receiueth his testimony:

33 He that hath receiued his testimonie, *hath set to his seale, that God is true.

34 For he whom God hath sent, speaketh the words of God: for God giueth not the Spirit by measure vnto him,

*Num. 21. 9.

*1. Iohn 4. 9.

*Chap. 12. 47.

*Chap. 1. 4.

||Or, discouered.

*Chap. 4. 2.

*Cha. 1. 7. 34.

*Hebr. 5. 4.
||Or, take vnto himselfe.

*Chap. 1. 20.

*Rom. 3. 4.

35 *The Father loueth the Sonne, and hath giuen all things into his hand.

36 *He that beleeueth on the Sonne, hath euerlasting life: and hee that beleeueth not the Sonne, shall not see life: but the wrath of God abideth on him.

CHAP. IIII.

1 Christ talketh with a woman of Samaria, and reuealeth himselfe vnto her. 27 His disciples marueile. 31 He declareth to them his zeale to Gods glory. 39 Many Samaritanes beleeue on him. 43 He departeth into Galile, and healeth the rulers sonne that lay sicke at Capernaum.

WHen therefore the Lord knew how the Pharisees had heard that Iesus made and baptized moe disciples then Iohn,

2 (Though Iesus himselfe baptized not, but his disciples:)

3 He left Iudea, and departed againe into Galile.

4 And he must needs goe thorow Samaria.

5 Then commeth hee to a citie of Samaria, which is called Sychar, neere to the parcell of ground, *that Iacob gaue to his sonne Ioseph.

6 Now Iacobs Well was there. Iesus therefore being wearied with his iourney, sate thus on the Well: & it was about the sixt houre.

7 There commeth a woman of Samaria to draw water: Iesus saith vnto her, Giue me to drinke.

8 For his disciples were gone away vnto the citie to buy meate.

9 Then saith the woman of Samaria vnto him, How is it that thou, being a Iew, askest drinke of me, which am a woman of Samaria? For the Iewes haue no dealings with the Samaritanes.

10 Iesus answered, and said vnto her, If thou knewest the gift of God, and who it is that saith to thee, Giue me to drinke: thou wouldest haue asked of him, and he would haue giuen thee liuing water.

11 The woman saith vnto him, Sir, thou hast nothing to draw with, & the Well is deepe: from whence then hast thou that liuing water?

12 Art thou greater then our father Iacob, which gaue vs the Well, and dranke thereof himselfe, and his children, and his cattell?

13 Iesus answered, and sayd vnto her, Whosoeuer drinketh of this water, shal thirst againe:

14 But whosoeuer drinketh of the water that I shall giue him, shall neuer thirst: but the water that I shall giue him, shall be in him a Well of water springing vp into euerlasting life.

15 The woman saith vnto him, Sir, giue me this water, that I thirst not, neither come hither to draw.

16 Iesus saith vnto her, Goe, call thy husband, and come hither.

17 The woman answered, and said, I haue no husband. Iesus saith vnto her, Thou hast well said, I haue no husband:

18 For thou hast had fiue husbands, and hee whom thou now hast, is not thy husband: In that saidest thou truely.

19 The woman saith vnto him, Sir, I perceiue that thou art a Prophet.

20 Our fathers worshipped in this mountaine, and yee say, that *in Hierusalem is the place where men ought to worship.

21 Iesus

*Matt. 11. 27.

*Habac. 2. 4.
1. iohn 5. 10.

*Gen. 33. 19.
and 48. 22.
iosh. 24. 23.

*Deut. 12. 5.

WEBOGRAPHY

Helpful websites for further research:

"AT-A-GLANCE" TIMETABLE:
http://www.xs4all.nl/~knops/timetab.html

BIBLE IN ENGLISH:
http://www.bible-researcher.com/versions.html

BIBLE TEXTS [IN GENERAL]:
http://www.bibletexts.com/bibliogr/02bib-hg.htm

BIBLICAL ARCHAEOLOGY:
http://www.bibleinterp.com/index.htm

CANON(S) OF HOLY SCRIPTURE (AND THE APOCRYPHA):
http://www.bible-researcher.com/canon.html

CATHOLIC ENCYCLOPEDIA ONLINE:
www.newadvent.org

CHURCH OF ENGLAND:
http://10.1911encyclopedia.org/E/EN/ENGLAND_CHURCH_OF.htm

CUNEIFORM:
http://www.eee.bham.ac.uk/cuneiform/

DOUAY-RHEIMS BIBLE:
http://www.geocities.com/Heartland/Acres/3964/bibles/noframes/douayrheims.html

DUKE UNIVERSITY PAPYRUS ARCHIVE:
http://scriptorium.lib.duke.edu/papyrus/

EARLY CHRISTIAN WRITINGS:
http://www.earlychristianwritings.com/

ISLAMIC INFORMATION ON NEW TESTAMENT MANUSCRIPTS:
http://www.islamic-awareness.org/Bible/Text/Mss/

ISRAEL ANTIQUITIES AUTHORITY:
http://www.israntique.org.il/

ISRAEL MUSEUM, JERUSALEM (THE SHRINE OF THE BOOK):
http://www.imj.org.il/eng/shrine/faq.html

JEWISH ENCYCLOPEDIA ONLINE:
http://www.jewishencyclopedia.com/index.jsp

Left: King James Bible page, pulpit folio edition

LIBRARY OF CONGRESS ON THE DEAD SEA SCROLLS:
http://lcweb.loc.gov/exhibits/scrolls/toc.html

LIBRARY OF CONGRESS ON THOMAS JEFFERSON & LIBERTY:
http://www.loc.gov/exhibits/jefferson/jeffworld.html

LOLLARD BIBLIOGRAPHY:
http://lollard.home.att.net/biblosec.html

PAPYROLOGY:
www.columbia.edu/cu/lweb/projects/digital/apis/index.html
http://cs-tr.cs.berkeley.edu/APIS/index.html
http://lhpc.arts.kuleuven.ac.be/

REINA-VALERA BIBLE (English and Spanish language sites on the Spanish Bible):
http://www.amen.net/lb/english/defensabrogdon.htm
http://clientes.vianetworks.es/personal/cer/Enciclo/reina.htm
http://www.labiblia.org/reinavalera_eng.htm
http://www.amen.net/lb/articulos/1569intro.htm

RYRIE COLLECTION:
http://www.smu.edu/bridwell/publications/ryrie_catalog/toc.htm

SEPTUAGINT:
http://students.cua.edu/16kalvesmaki/lxx/
http://ccat.sas.upenn.edu/ioscs/commentary/prospectus.html

TYNDALE, WILLIAM:
http://www.williamtyndale.com/index.html

WEST SEMITIC RESEARCH PROJECT AT UNIVERSITY OF SOUTHERN CALIFORNIA:
http://www.usc.edu/dept/LAS/wsrp/index.html

MEMORABLE WORDS ON GOD, THE BIBLE, AND AMERICA

"So great is my veneration for the Bible that the earlier my children begin to read it, the more confident will be my hope that they will prove useful citizens to their country, and respectable members of society."

JOHN QUINCY ADAMS (1767–1848)
Sixth President of the U.S.

"Here before me is the Bible used in the inauguration of our first president, in 1789, and I have taken the oath of office on the Bible my mother gave me, opened to a timeless admonition from the ancient prophet Micah: 'He hath showed thee, O man, what is good; and what doth the Lord require of thee, but to do justly, and to love mercy, and to walk humbly with thy God.'"

JIMMY CARTER (1924 –)
39th President of the U.S.
Inaugural Address, January 20, 1977

"Must everything in our age be pre-digested? Does the Bible have to be reduced to pablum? I refuse to believe that modern man, who split the atom and is exploring space, is unable to cope with the grandeur and glory of the King James Version."

WINSTON S. CHURCHILL (1874–1965)
British Prime Minister

"I have lived, sir, a long time, and the longer I live, the more convincing proofs I see of this truth: that God governs the affairs of men. If a sparrow cannot fall to the ground without his notice, is it probable that an empire can rise without his aid? We have been assured, sir, in the Sacred Writings, that except the Lord build the house they labor in vain that build it."

BENJAMIN FRANKLIN (1706–1790)

"It is impossible to mentally or socially enslave a Bible-reading people. The principles of the Bible are the groundwork of human freedom."

HORACE GREELEY (1811–1872)

"My friends, before I begin the expression of those thoughts that I deem appropriate to this moment, would you permit me the privilege of uttering a little private prayer of my own. And I ask that you bow your heads. 'Almighty God, as we stand here at this moment, my future associates in the executive branch of government join me in beseeching that Thou will make full and complete our dedication to the service of the people in this throng and their fellow citizens everywhere. Give us, we pray, the power to discern clearly right from wrong, and allow all our words and actions to be governed thereby, and by the laws of this land. Especially we pray that our concern shall be for all people regardless of station, race, or calling. May cooperation be permitted and be the mutual aim of those who, under the concepts of our Constitution, hold to differing political faiths; so that all may work for the good of our beloved country and Thy glory, Amen.'"

DWIGHT D. EISENHOWER (1890–1969)
34th President of the U.S.
First Inaugural Address, January 20, 1953

"Hold fast to the Bible as the sheet-anchor of your liberties; write its precepts in your hearts and practice them in your lives."

ULYSSES S. GRANT (1822–1885)
18th President of the U.S.

"It cannot be emphasized too strongly or too often that this great nation was founded, not by religionists, but by Christians...not on religions, but on the Gospel of Jesus Christ."

PATRICK HENRY (1736–1799)

"The whole inspiration of our civilization springs from the teachings of Christ and the lessons of the prophets. To read the Bible for these fundamentals is a necessity of American life."

HERBERT HOOVER (1874–1964)
31st President of the U.S.

"The Bible is the source of Liberty."
THOMAS JEFFERSON (1743–1826)
Third President of the U.S.

60

"The Bible, sir, is the Rock upon which our Republic rests."

ANDREW JACKSON (1767–1845)
Seventh President of the U.S.

"The same revolutionary beliefs for which our forebears fought are still at issue around the globe—the beliefs that the rights of man come not from the generosity of the state, but from the hand of God."

JOHN FITZGERALD KENNEDY (1917–1963)
35th President of the U.S.
Inaugural Address, January 20, 1961

"The first question which the priest and the Levite asked was: 'If I stop to help this man, what will happen to me?' But the Good Samaritan reversed the question: 'If I do not stop to help this man, what will happen to him?'"

MARTIN LUTHER KING, JR. (1929–1968)
Civil Rights Pioneer

"We have been the recipients of the choicest bounties of heaven. We have been preserved these many years in peace and prosperity. We have grown in numbers, wealth and power, as no other nation has ever grown. But we have forgotten God. We have forgotten the gracious hand which preserved us in peace, and multiplied and enriched and strengthened us; and we have vainly imagined, in the deceitfulness of our hearts, that all these blessings were produced by some superior wisdom and virtue of our own. Intoxicated with unbroken success, we have become too self-sufficient to feel the necessity of redeeming and preserving grace, too proud to pray to the God that made us!"

ABRAHAM LINCOLN (1809–1865)
16th President of the U.S.

"The philosophy of the school room in one generation will be the philosophy of the government in the next."

ABRAHAM LINCOLN (1809–1865)
16th President of the U.S.

61

"I am much afraid that schools will prove to be the great gates of hell unless they diligently labor in explaining the Holy Scripture, engraving them in the hearts of youth. I advise no one to place his child where the Scriptures do not reign paramount."

MARTIN LUTHER (1483–1546)
Founder of the German Reformation Movement

"We have staked the whole future of American civilization, not upon the power of government, far from it. We have staked the future of all our political institutions upon the capacity of mankind for self-government; upon the capacity of each and all of us to govern ourselves, to control ourselves, to sustain ourselves according to the Ten Commandments of God."

JAMES MADISON (1751–1836)
Fourth President of the U.S.

"We will either be governed by God or ruled by tyrants."
WILLIAM PENN (1644–1718)

"I am told that tens of thousands of prayer meetings are being held on this day, and for that I am deeply grateful. We are a nation under God, and I believe God intended for us to be free. It would be fitting and good, I think, if on each inauguration day in future years it should be declared a day of prayer."

RONALD REAGAN (1911–2004)
40th President of the U.S.
First Inaugural Address, January 20, 1981

"Voltaire expected that within fifty years of his lifetime there would not be one Bible in the world. His house is now a distribution center for Bibles in many languages."

CORRIE TEN BOOM (1892–1983)

"I enter a most earnest plea that in our hurried and rather bustling life of today we do not lose the hold our forefathers had on the Bible."

THEODORE ROOSEVELT (1858–1919)
26th President of the U.S.

"It is impossible rightly to govern the world without God and the Bible."

GEORGE WASHINGTON (1732–1799)
First President of the U.S.

"I sought for the greatness of America in her harbors and rivers and fertile fields, and her mines and commerce. It was not there. Not until I went into the Churches and heard her pulpits flame with righteousness did I understand the greatness of her power. America is great because she is good; and if America ever ceases to be good, America will cease to be great."

ALEXIS DE TOCQUEVILLE (1805–1859)
From *Democracy in America*

"The Bible is our only safe guide. The Bible fits man for life and prepares him for death."

DANIEL WEBSTER (1782–1852)
American Statesman

"The Bible is for the Government of the People, by the People, and for the People."

JOHN WYCLIF (c. 1320–1384)
First Translator of the English Bible

ABOUT THE AUTHOR

Lee Biondi is Co-Curator of rarities in the new exhibition, *From the Dead Sea Scrolls to the Bible in America*.

Mr. Biondi has lectured at churches, schools, and special events on many aspects of the history of Scripture from antiquity to modern America. He has been interviewed by dozens of newspapers on these topics and has appeared on numerous radio and television shows.

Mr. Biondi is still widely recognized as one of today's leading private dealers and consultants in Rare Books and Manuscripts, with a specialization in Ancient and Medieval Biblical Manuscripts and Early Printed Bibles. This unusual background has provided unprecedented access to some of the world's finest private collections. This has been a boon to the assembling of a unique collection covering the story of the Scriptures.

For more than a decade, Mr. Biondi was manager of the largest and most successful antiquarian book store in the country, The Heritage Book Shop in Los Angeles, where he specialized in rare manuscript and printed Bibles, and first editions of Charles Dickens and James Joyce. He left that role in 2001 to become a private dealer and consultant to major collectors. He is a published author on the bibliographies and biographies of Dickens, Joyce, Edgar Allan Poe, Anthony Trollope, Jules Verne, Boris Pasternak, Ian Fleming, Victorian Women Novelists, and *The Arabian Nights* in Arabic, French and English. Mr. Biondi entered the world of Rare Books in 1990 from the corporate world of new books, having spent years in Los Angeles handling West Coast retail divisions for Crown Books and Doubleday.

Raised Presbyterian by his Roman Catholic father and Southern Baptist mother, Mr. Biondi is now non-denominational.